How to Make Money Online:
Create a $10,000 Per Month Business while on Vacation

Brendan Mace

Table of Contents

FREE BONUS: Simple Two Step Formula

Click Here to Get Your FREE Bonus

Find this Bonus Here: http://TwoStep.BrendanMace.com

This bonus is a 3-part video series that shows the process I've used to make $5,000/month.

In reality, my income since creating the video series has actually increased even further. I am now happy to make "Five Figures Per Month"

Whether you like reading or watching a video, I have you covered. My personal preference is to do both, and I recommend you use whatever learning style helps you the most.

I have an entire YouTube channel with 90+ videos on "making money online"

Over 19,000 people are subscribed to my channel, and many have figured this game out.

Join my tribe here: https://youtube.com/user/macbr9

Introduction

I used to work at Boston Pizza for $10.25 per hour.

Education left me over $30,000 in debt.

When I Google searched "What to do with a Sociology degree?" the first result I found said to "Frame it on the wall."

I was trying hard to get a job, even though the idea of spending years in one place terrified me.

You can work hard every day in your life, but that's not going to make you a millionaire.

The only way to ensure that your efforts will directly impact your earnings is to become an entrepreneur.

As I learned from my first "real job," working hard for somebody else's dollar is a fool's game.

How in the hell
could a man enjoy being awakened at 6:30 a.m. by an alarm clock, leap out of bed, dress, force-feed, shit, piss, brush teeth and hair, and fight traffic to get to a place where essentially you made lots of money for somebody else and were asked to be grateful for the opportunity to do so?
- Charles Bukowski, *Factotum*, 1975

I decided three years ago that my life was not going to be normal.

What I needed to know was, "How in the hell" could I quit the rat race.

That's when I stumbled across a guide that screamed "Make $5,000/month in your pajamas."

I don't remember the exact title, or the exact claims. But the essence was "Make Money Online" with no effort.

Like a drug addict to a cocaine baggie -- I was hooked.

While still employed at Boston Pizza, I would come home late at night and stay awake dreaming about business.

The idea of becoming wealthy was enough to keep me satisfied, but my business was not growing.

The guide I purchased was Bullshit.

… And I learned why.

It claimed that making money online was easy. Worse than that, it practically said "no effort."

That's a red flag.

Anyone that says they can teach you how to make the big bucks with no effort deserves exactly zero seconds of your precious time.

If making money online were really that easy, a hell of a lot more people would be doing it.

The former richest man in the world, Warren Buffet, wisely shares "In Business, I look for economic castles protected by unbreachable moats."

The goal is not easy. It's about doing ***one thing*** better than your competitors.

Click here to claim your free coaching call:

https://docs.google.com/forms/d/1QsQ7mWtyLWhoyqwfvT4FBiUCope0vynz8Dzgy1-53HA/viewform

My journey has had many ups and downs along the way. I learned from my MANY mistakes and have fine-tuned a system that is simple, passive and duplicatable.

After eight years of struggling to make this work, I now make about $10,000 every month with a business that I could teach to a ten year old.

That's why at the end of 2015 I opened the doors to the **Brendan Mace coaching program**.

Many students are now making this online thing a full time gig.

That means that people are done with the BS and are ready to quit jobs and live a better life. It may sound far-fetched now, but get your own free **coaching call here**, and I can show you exactly how this is possible.

Sure, it felt really good to change my own life a couple years ago, but there's been nothing more rewarding than duplicating my success with dozens of my peers.

No longer do you have to work a job you hate. Or pass up a vacation opportunity because you don't have the money to enjoy your life.

I am confident this guide will give you new ideas and perspectives on how to build a business.

I am not a rocket scientist.

I built a $10,000/month online business and I will show you exactly how I did it.

Don't let the price of this book fool you. This is the real blueprint I use to make a living online.

Treat it like an expensive course and you will maximize the value you get from it.

What would happen if you don't take action on this book?

Absolutely nothing.

For many of us, that's the problem.

Three years ago, I needed a change. My debt was growing while jobs were sparse.

I graduated university, and I still felt like a failure.

While I agree with the cliché "money doesn't buy happiness." I still strongly believe that poverty buys a whole lot of stress and uncertainty.

Deciding to learn this business model is the change I needed.

To think, if I had given up, I could still be working for $10.25 per hour.

You can have a better life.

Let me show you how!

Chapter 1 – Worst Mistakes

The secret to making money online is passive income.

The problem is how to build it.

A very wise marketer once told me "you just need to make $2 for every $1 you spend."

I like that message. While business plans can all too often be overwhelmingly complicated with graphs, charts and accountants, at the end of the day, what matters most is that you make more than you spend.

The only flaw in that logic is that focusing on the <u>investment to profit</u> ratio encourages hoarding money rather than investing.

After all, if you're not spending money, it's a hell of a lot easier to make more than you spend. Keeping your money in the piggy bank, though, won't grow a business.

Untie the purse strings because you can't cheap your way to success. You may have less expenses making money online than you would with a brick and mortar shop. However, avoiding spending any money is one of the biggest mistakes you can make.

In fact, most successful entrepreneurs spend crap-loads of money; the crux though is that they make more than they spend. Understand that principle, and you can become very wealthy.

The best way to have a high profit margin is to create a passive income stream.

The common tragedy of wannabe entrepreneurs is that they pump all their investment into one-off money making strategies.

An example of this is the most basic level of affiliate marketing.

Too many affiliates send traffic directly to an offer using their "affiliate link," and while any sales generated by that link benefits this affiliate, he has a lottery ticket's chance in hell of making consistent Income.

In a perfect world, the affiliate would buy traffic and make more money from affiliate sales than the costs encumbered.

Unfortunately, the more likely scenario is that this affiliate earns in commissions nowhere even close to the amount he spends.

He grumbles. He complains. He tells everyone that making money online is a scam.

What this "Short Sighted Steven" doesn't realize is that he could have made money (a lot of it), if he had just created a funnel instead.

The Solution – Passive Profit

Instead of looking for an immediate return, the better option is to collect money over time.

Short Sighted Steven would have been much better off collecting an email address first.

If Steven really needed some quick cash, he could still redirect new subscribers to an offer anyways. Which would give him the best of both worlds. An opportunity to make money right off the top, as well as a customer base he can tap into for years to come.

Without a doubt, the best way to make money online is with passive income.

There are a few ways to build a sustainable online business, but one of the easiest and fastest ways is list building.

For that reason, this book will focus on making money online with an email list.

Warning: This business model creates "traffic on tap." A smart reader will use this free traffic to make consistent money every single day of the week. Please ignore this guide if you hate money.

Chapter 2 – How it Works

List building without a plan is like speed dating with no clothes on.

Sure, the odd person may subscribe out of pity.

If you want long-term success, though, you need to have the right approach.

In this book, I'll show you how _my blueprint_ built a relationship with 42,390 people using the SAME predictable system.

Over and over again…

What you could do with 42,390 subscribers?

Imagine what you could do with this many subscribers.

My name is Brendan Mace, and I run www.BrendanMace.com and the Brendan Mace YouTube channel and this the story of how I built a list of over 40K subscribers in less than 20 minutes per day, without spending a dime from my own pocket.

Each day I take 10-20 minutes to email my list.

In that time, I almost always make at least 5 sales.

These commissions range from:

- Measly $9 sales.
- $200+ high-ticket commissions.

All-in, I'm currently getting about $3,500-4000/Month from list building.

Remember, I only spend about 15 minutes per day on this stuff.

With that money, I could:

- Support my family
- Pay rent, utilities, etc.
- Not have a job
- No boss
- Learn a new skill
- Read
- Travel

I'll be honest and say that I love ALL these options, but my personal focus has been on traveling.

In the last 6 months, I've been to:

- The Okanagan
- Las Vegas

- Cuba
- Mexico
- Colombia

Here's a pic of me partying in Colombia:

I'm the dude that's tanked on the right.

It's a tough life. Lol!

As I write this blog post, the misses and I are planning a trip to the Dominican Republic.

The reality is that when you trade dollars for pesos, you really don't need that much online income to achieve your dreams.

And you really don't have to waste your life in a cubicle.

10-20 minutes per day is all you need for the "laptop lifestyle"

Chapter 3 – The Instant Offer

Any successful email marketer will tell you the same thing…

Building a list costs money.

Don't worry, though.

If you set this up right, then you aren't really spending anything out of your own pocket.

The goal is to create a funnel that _covers all your costs for you._

So that the whole thing is virtually free.

How do you create a system that pays for itself?

The key is an <u>instant offer</u>

What I mean by "instant" is that an offer is presented immediately after a subscriber opts-in.

We'll discuss the importance of this in a second…

The best instant offers are products that are cheap and appeal to impulse

I know you've probably heard a thousand times to AVOID promoting cheap products.

I've even heard the ludicrous claim that "high-ticket products convert the same as low-ticket items"

If this logic were true, then promoting high-ticket stuff would be a no brainer.

It's NOT true.

Nobody is going to buy a high-ticket product from someone they just met.

Not going to happen.

You should promote mid-to-high ticket stuff at some point in your funnel.

BUT, not on a first encounter.

That's like a stranger on the street asking you to buy a $25,000 Honda.

He'd be <u>much more likely</u> to sell me a $5 glass of lemonade.

Even though he'd make WAYYYY more selling a $25,000 product. Nobody's going to buy it.

This logic holds true for new subscribers.

Your _instant offer_ should be in the $7-$27 price range.

That's a cost that can be justified on impulse.

People drop $7-10 on expensive lattes on the daily.

Spending less than 10 bucks on a course or blueprint is non-threatening.

Many will buy just because they are bored.

How are we going to make anything off this?

You may be thinking, only $7-27 per sale. That's peanuts.

How the heck do we get rich???

Upsells my friend.

Most MMO products have additional offers after the initial sale.

These upsells are targeted at people that have already made a purchase. The conversion rate on these is much higher than average.

Let's say, for example, that a new subscriber buys your instant offer for $9.

Cool!

$9 is still money in your pocket.

That same new subscriber is now shown FOUR upsells.

Each with an average cost of $20.

Let's say he buys just *two of these upsells.*

This one new subscriber has now given you $49 in commissions.

And it all started with a cheap easy-to-buy $9 instant offer.

Brendan, show me an example

A $9.95 instant offer that I use for my main funnel is called "Copy. Paste. Hack."

Here's a pic:

Copy & Paste My $58,491 Per Month Campaigns & Start Using Them For Yourself...

Let's Skip The B.S. & Get Straight To It. You Want To Make Money Online & I Can Help You Do It...

Take a look at the message in the main headline.

Desmond is saying, "Copy and paste your way to $58,491"

We want to attract impulsive buyers, remember?

This tells visitors that they can make a ton of money.

… And it only costs them $9.95 to learn how.

Of course, most visitors are not going to believe a word of it. We all know that it's not as easy as *copy and paste* to build that kind of income.

But heck… It's $9.95

The dream alone is worth that price and more.

Thought experiment:

Imagine you purchased a 500 click solo ad.

The vendor ended up sending you 542 unique clicks. What a nice guy…

Let's say that your guru-style squeeze page nets a cool 50% of visitors into new subscribers.

(More on this later…)

So of your 542 visitors – you gain round a 'bout 271 new subscribers.

Those 271 new subs are redirected to your instant offer.

Let's say it's <u>Copy. Paste. Hack.</u>

How many subscribers need to buy your instant offer in order for you to make a profit?

Let's say the average sale nets you $29, and the solo ad costs $150

$29 is the initial sale + one upsell.

Remember, the visitor here is offered 4 upsells.

Some will buy two. Some will buy one. Some will be none.

That means, that out of 271 people, you need to make 5 sales.

5 sales = $145

… Around the price of your solo.

That's a conversion rate of only 1.8%

The average conversion rate of Copy. Paste. Hack. is 5.0%

Over DOUBLE what you need to break even…

Does that mean I'm rich?

Not yet…

The one upsell per sale might be a bit generous.

And there will certainly be some refunds.

… That's unavoidable.

What this does demonstrate is that it's realistic to (at least) "break even"

If you break even on the front end – you win.

This is only taking into account whether you make your money back right away.

Most of your BIG money will come on the back end.

Let's talk about that now…

Chapter 4 – The Back End

The back end of your funnel is your auto responder sequence.

This is where you do three things:

- Build trust
- Get traffic to your stuff
- Make big $$$

The first few emails should focus on providing value.

Subscribers will only buy from you if they trust your recommendations.

If you pitch stuff ALL the time, without adding value, your subs will notice.

My email sequence is 150+ emails

That mixes in value and promotions. Meaning that subscribers trust you, and then buy from you.

You can steal this whole funnel in the next 10 minutes

In only 2 steps...

1 Sign up to Aweber (Free 30-day Trial)
2 Paste in this Campaign Share Code: awlist3794060-a1f00-$F

Aweber allows "one-click" sharing of auto responder emails.

Good on 'em.

If you'd prefer to create the sequence yourself, then make sure you loosely follow this formula.

Emails 1-8

- Mostly add value. Maybe 1-3 promotions MAX.

Emails 9-20

  • Mixture of 50/50. Half value. Half promotions.

Emails 21-150

  • Mostly promotions. Mine's about 75% promo w/ 25% value-based.

… And that's it

After email 20, your subscribers already know what you're about.

Plus, you're still sending them something of value almost TWICE per week.

That's far ahead of what other marketers are doing. And it will grossly improve your ROI when you do actually promote stuff.

How often should I email?

Every. Damn. Day.

"There's only one thing worse than being talked about, and that's not being talked about."

The moral of this quote is you want people to be talking or thinking about you.

This is especially true in MMO. Subscribers are usually on a dozen or more email lists. They have a limited supply of attention – if you're emailing less than three times a week, most subs will forget you exist.

Yes, some subscribers are going to hate your guts.

That will be the minority – and it's inevitable.

No matter what you do in MMO. There will be a herd of people that think you're a liar.

I've published dozens of YouTube tutorials that just share what I do on a certain topic.

For example, "how to build Twitter followers" or "how to create a niche site from scratch"

These tutorials make me very little.

They were not created to make money. I filmed them to build a relationship. To add value with my audience.

Nothing malicious about that – and yet I get comments daily that tell me to F#$K OFF

It's strange – but it's the reality we live in.

Don't take it personally. If you're providing value to your subscribers, these haters will eventually find someone new to blast profanities at.

Email Daily. Some will love you for it.

Most importantly. More subscribers will <u>notice YOU.</u>

Be noticeable!

Chapter 5 – The Landing Page

The best way to get subscribers is with a landing page.

Sure, a blog could snag a bunch of subscribers for free. Which is all fine and dandy, but the conversion rates are shockingly low. A good blogging set up *converts only 3-5% of visitors* into subscribers.

That's peanuts!

A good landing page converts over 50% of visitors into your email subs.

That's more than 10X the conversion rate from a blog.

A landing page DEMANDS attention to your offer.

Here's an example: http://twostep.brendanmace.com

My first landing page SUCKED…

I spent the better part of my weekend, scratching through the HTML code. Figuring out how to create a headline.

Excited to finally launch it, my expectations were massive.

It looked cool to me…

The conversion was less than 20%

Then, my marketing buddy that I chat with on Skype from time-to-time said, "why are you building these pages from scratch?"

There are about a dozen solid Landing Page Creators that do most of the work for you.

So I decided to check them out.

I bought all of them: Lead Pages, Landing Page Monkey, ClickFunnels, etc.

My favorite, by far, is WP Profit Builder

- It's much cheaper (only a one-time payment)
- Copies proven winners (guaranteed results)
- Easy to use (no more geeky code)

Here are some of the pages you can set up in the next 10 minutes:

Attention grabber!

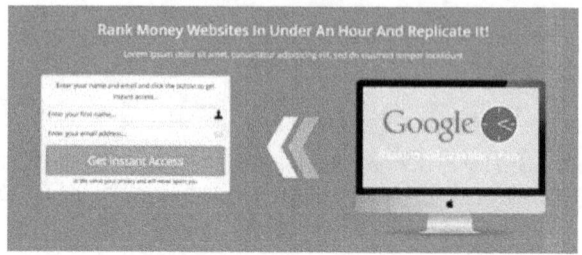

Good for FREE EBooks!

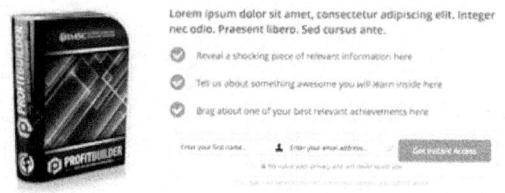

All-time favorite!

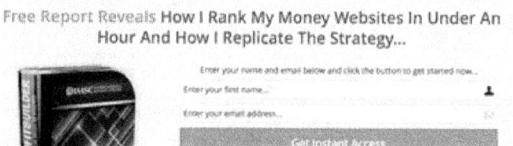

That pic look familiar?

It's the exact same template that I use with my main squeeze funnel.

With some minor changes. All in – took me 5-10 minutes!

… And now I have a landing page that converts at 55.6%

All I did was change the text and toss up a picture of me my beautiful girlfriend.

Here's the final result:

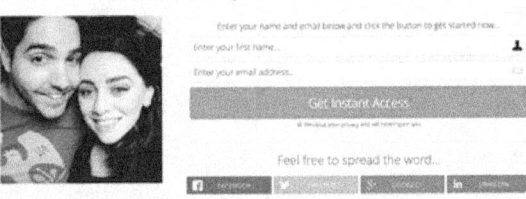

Simple 2-Step Formula Earns me over $146.72 in 12 Hours. This is Weird, But it Works!

That leads me to my next point.

Make it <u>personal</u>

There are so many marketers that find an eBook, and think it'll convert like no other.

This is 2015 people!!

Nobody cares about your crappy 10-page thoughts on setting up a Twitter profile.

Sorry to be blunt.

I used to be all over eBooks, and how to give them away for leads.

Think about it – *does a virtual book excite you?*

Probably not.

What excites people is

- Changing their life
- Quitting their job
- Providing for the family

They want the dream.

It's near impossible to convey those excitements in a virtual book.

What about a video, or a personalized course?

Now we're getting somewhere!

Who says you need to give something away?

The "typical" way to build a list is to give a freebie away.

… You don't have to do this, though. You still have a choice.

Although it's less popular to promote something right off the bat. It can be immensely profitable to do so.

Chapter 6 – Free Traffic or Cash

There are two ways to promote from the start

I mean, there are probably a thousand ways. But here's the two that are most effective.

1) Promote an Offer

This one's self-explanatory. The landing page building excitement and anticipation for a course, instead of a freebie of some sort. This is usually more profitable, but breeds less goodwill with your subscribers.

2) Send direct traffic to your click trading partners.

This one is definitely controversial, but it's one way to damn near guarantee (supposing that you have a good landing page) that you can get free traffic on autopilot.

In the next step, I'll be discussing traffic.

Part of our traffic strategy is to trade clicks with marketing friends.

This means that we send 200 or so clicks to our buddy. We'll call him "Mike."

Once Mike gets our traffic, he sends back 200 clicks to our offer.

One way to get the 200 clicks to Mike is to promote his squeeze page right after a subscriber opts-in.

Let's say your squeeze page converts at 55%.

That means, that on a solo ad, approximately half the visitors will subscribe AND see Mike's offer.

So on a 200-click solo, we get 105 subscribers, and 105 clicks to our traffic partner.

Let's not to stop there…

- We bought 200 clicks.
- We gained 105 subscribers.
- We sent 105 clicks to Mike's page.

We still need 95 more clicks to Mike's page in order to get our original solo all reinvested in another traffic source.

The first email should get about a 50% open rate.

If we put Mike's offer in the next follow-up email, and feature his offer as a main link, we could reasonably expect 20% of new subscribers to click it.

That means an extra 20 clicks.

Now, if our next 10 emails get a 20% open rate average.

And we feature Mike's link in those emails…

We can expect maybe 6-10% of subscribers to click Mike's link in EACH of those messages.

105 subscribers X 10 Emails X 8%

That's 84 clicks to Mike's offer.

Now let's count our outgoing traffic.

Number of Out Going Clicks:

- 105 Clicks directly after opt-in
- 20 Clicks from first email clicks
- 84 Clicks from email 2-11

Total clicks = 209

Ta da!!!

In 11 days, we have *fully recouped* the 200 click solo ad

Any further clicks, or affiliate sales are pure profit.

Now, Mike owes us 209 clicks. And the process repeats as before.

Instead of Mike, we'll need to find someone new to trade clicks with.

That's where step #4 comes in….

Step #4 – Getting Traffic for Free

My favorite traffic source is solo ads.

They're:

- Easy
- Affordable
- Predictable

If you have a landing page that averages 50% opt-in, pretty much every solo ad will result in between 40-65% opt-in rate.

If it's lower or higher than that – something's not right about it.

In general, if a solo's results are terrible, a good solo vendor will compensate you in some way.

So in 99% of cases, Solo ads are predictably lucrative.

Even with a 40% opt-in rate, you can still make money. A lot of money.

So, your traffic solution is simple.

Buy traffic for cheap, and make more than you spend.

The best place to find cheap solo ads is on FaceBook.

… And best of all, it's free.

Load up FaceBook, and search for "solo ads"

Here's a group right here: https://www.facebook.com/groups/189347897917735/

There are at least a dozen FB groups for solo ads. All filled with hundreds or thousands of members.

Take a look through these groups, and find someone that has a proven reputation.

There's no formula for finding solo sellers. Just use your common sense.

A good seller has:

- Lots of testimonials
- Very few (if any) people upset with their services

There are LOADS of good sellers on FB. And many of them are willing to sell for cheap.

My recommendation is to HAGGLE.

No solo ad price is set in stone. You can contact ANY of these sellers, and ask for a better price.

I know of two sellers that I've talked down from .40/click to .25/click.

That's almost a 50% off savings.

Usually you won't snag that big a discount. But more sellers than not will set to you for a cheaper price.

The most important rule…

KISS – Keep it Simple Stupid

- Buy solo ads cheap
- Make money
- Build subscribers
- Reinvest profits

With those simple 4-step bullets, you could build an entire business.

There's no reason to complicate any of this.

Buy for cheap. Make more than you spend!

Solo ads typically cost about .40/click.

Many sell higher than that price, but some will list lower than that.

Haggling, and smart investing, could easily bump your average traffic cost down to .30/click.

I have a half dozen solo sellers that give me traffic for .25 per click. Finding these sellers is very doable.

If you get a solo ad for .25 per click, and 50% opt-in to your list, you only need to make 50 cents per subscriber to break even.

That's ludicrously reasonable.

Get the potential yet??

Breaking even means building a list for free.

Chapter 7 – The Real Money

There are a million things you can do with your email list.

But here's the main two:

Trading clicks with partners.

Looking at the EXACT same FB groups from earlier, we can find LOADS of partners.

Trading clicks is easy.

> 1) Find people willing to trade
> 2) Send traffic to their offers

The best way to do this is to set up what's called a "link rotator."

In geek talk, this is where you have a single link that rotates from one banking partner to the next.

The benefit of a rotator is that you can set up click deals with 4-20+ partners, and let the traffic unroll on autopilot.

Let's say you have 4 trading partners.

> • The first deal is worth 500 clicks
> • Second is for 300
> • Third, 100 again
> • And the fourth is for 150

It can be really challenging to ensure that you send the right amount of traffic to each of these partners.

You don't want to send too little to any one. But almost as bad as that is sending too much. It's bad for the ROI.

With a link rotator, it will send 500 clicks to the first trading partner. Once it reaches that number (that you set) it rotates to the next partner. It will finish those clicks before moving on to the third partner. And so on….

Pretty cool, huh?

It takes care of your whole traffic management for you.

The best tool that I've seen that does this (and much more) is called ClickMagick.

It will:

> 1 Rotate links
> 2 Track number of clicks

3 Tell you if traffic is real or fake
4 Tell you traffic quality

There are many features that I'm leaving out here. Trust me, ClickMagick really saves a lot of time, and makes you more money.

That being said, if you are determined to use a shoestring budget, there are free trackers available.

Services, like Bit.Ly offer a free link tracker.

I've never heard of a free link rotator. And Bit.Ly does not have the features of ClickMagick. But it will do the basic task of tracking clicks well. Which is all you 100% need out of a tracker.

Why are trading clicks profitable?

Because you can still make all the money you would have with a solo ad – except this time, the traffic is free.

So if your funnel makes $1 per subscriber, then a 200 click solo ad will make you $100 (with a 50% opt-in rate).

Traffic from trading partners can still get you the $1/subscriber.

… But this time without any costs. It's pure profit.

The instant offer + back end is just a free ride of affiliate commissions.

Promoting Stuff

The second main way to make money from your list is to promote stuff.

Simple concept. You have subscribers. They trust you. Recommend stuff. Make money.

To do this, sign up an account at ClickBank, Jvzoo and WarriorPlus

These websites have thousands of products to promote.

Pick the ones that look the best, get your affiliate link, and send an email to your list

You could easily create an email promotion for an offer in the next 10 minutes.

With a 30,000 subscriber email list, that would lead to a lot of affiliate commissions.

Any time you want money, you just send an offer to your list.

I have a phrase for this:

"Money on tap"

That's what it's like to have an email list.

- Need rent bills paid
- Flights/vacations booked
- Debt paid off
- Retirement

Press send on your email list. Collect the money.

It's really that simple.

Where to go from here?

Follow these 5 steps.

Bookmark this page, and work on a new step each day.

Rome wasn't built in a day. And your sales funnel won't be, either.

Within a week, you could have the whole thing ready to collect leads and profits on autopilot.

Always test!

So what if you've created a _landing page that converts at 38%?_

Making small changes to a sales funnel makes a BIG difference overall.

A 10% swing in either direction could determine whether you make money or not. The only way to have positive swings is to keep testing your results.

And Finally!

Enjoy your life.

Chapter 8 – Reaping the Benefits

The benefit of creating these funnels is that you have an income stream that grows while you sleep. You do NOT have to waste all your precious daylight hours in front of a screen.

- Go outside.
- Take your family on trips.
- Learn a new language.

With the extra time granted from a laptop lifestyle, the possibilities are endless.

New adventures are my favorite way to invest time.

You may feel awkward vacationing long term at first. The very idea conflicts with everything you've been told.

From childhood I was raised to believe that you work hard, and then every once in a while you can treat yourself to a short vacation.

I know people that have been working for thirty years, and they still fondly talk about that trip they took in there twenties.

While I'm glad they had a good time then, there's no reason why they can't live the "good life" permanently.

I've been travelling for the last ten months.

The most recent adventure was South East Asia.

Here's a picture of me on vacation:

What you can't see in that photo is the beach.

This adventure was on Ko Phagnan Island on the east side of Thailand.

You know what I've learned from my months of travelling?

Online business only takes me about 10-20 minutes per day.

The majority of the list building business model is automated.

In other words, if you put in a reasonable amount of work now, you can relax later.

I'm 28 years young, and I will never have to worry about a bill again in my life. But even further to that, I won't have to work another day either.

Making money online gives a whole new wrinkle to my previous "Work hard - Play hard" mindset.

Create yourself a passive income stream, and you can play a hell of a lot longer than you work.

Conclusion

This list building guide covers everything you need to know.

There are no underground secrets. You don't have to be a rocket scientist.

By taking action on *these 5 steps,* you can create an income stream that will change your life.

To watch over my shoulder and see it all done in video, check out my 3-Part YouTube series right here on this exact blueprint. You'll see everything over my shoulder as I go through the entire process.

I believe in you! You should too!

My last piece of advice is this: What we fear doing most is usually what we most need to do.

If you want to learn more about how to change your life with list building, then I would love to help you.

Head over to the homepage of my blog to see more in depth guides like this one.

Right here: www.brendanmace.com

www.ingramcontent.com/pod-product-compliance
Lightning Source LLC
Chambersburg PA
CBHW070427190526
45169CB00003B/1451